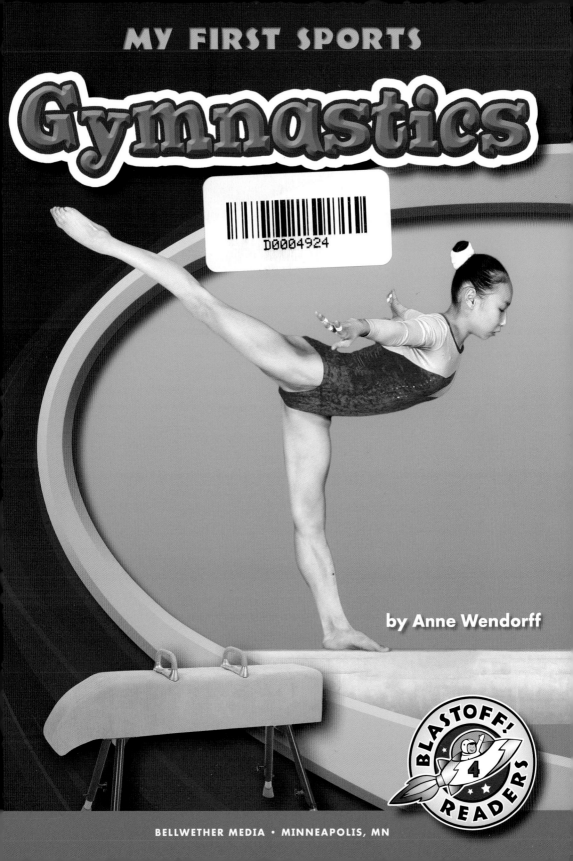

MY FIRST SPORTS

Gymnastics

by Anne Wendorff

BLASTOFF! READERS 4

BELLWETHER MEDIA • MINNEAPOLIS, MN

Note to Librarians, Teachers, and Parents:

Blastoff! Readers are carefully developed by literacy experts and combine standards-based content with developmentally appropriate text.

Level 1 provides the most support through repetition of high-frequency words, light text, predictable sentence patterns, and strong visual support.

Level 2 offers early readers a bit more challenge through varied simple sentences, increased text load, and less repetition of high-frequency words.

Level 3 advances early-fluent readers toward fluency through increased text and concept load, less reliance on visuals, longer sentences, and more literary language.

Level 4 builds reading stamina by providing more text per page, increased use of punctuation, greater variation in sentence patterns, and increasingly challenging vocabulary.

Level 5 encourages children to move from "learning to read" to "reading to learn" by providing even more text, varied writing styles, and less familiar topics.

Whichever book is right for your reader, Blastoff! Readers are the perfect books to build confidence and encourage a love of reading that will last a lifetime!

This edition first published in 2010 by Bellwether Media, Inc.

No part of this publication may be reproduced in whole or in part without written permission of the publisher. For information regarding permission, write to Bellwether Media, Inc., Attention: Permissions Department, 5357 Penn Avenue South, Minneapolis, MN 55419.

Library of Congress Cataloging-in-Publication Data
Wendorff, Anne.
  Gymnastics / by Anne Wendorff.
    p. cm. – (Blastoff! readers. My first sports)
  Includes bibliographical references and index.
  Summary: "Simple text and full-color photographs introduce beginning readers to the sport of gymnastics. Developed by literacy experts for students in grades two through five"–Provided by publisher.
  ISBN 978-1-60014-327-4 (hardcover : alk. paper)
  1. Gymnastics–Juvenile literature. I. Title.

  GV461.3.W46 2009
  796.44–dc22   2009008181

Printed in the United States of America, North Mankato, MN.   090110   1174

Contents

What Is Gymnastics?

Gymnastics is a sport involving the strength, balance, and **flexibility** of the human body. It often includes pieces of equipment that help a gymnast perform. It is practiced all over the world.

Gymnastics was created by Friedrich Ludwig Jahn in Germany in the 1800s. He opened a gym where he created and taught the moves of the new sport.

Jahn invented many pieces of gymnastics equipment, including the **balance beam**, the **high bar**, the **parallel bars**, and the **vault**. He taught men how to balance, swing, and jump off of this equipment. These exercises made the men strong and flexible.

The Basic Rules of Gymnastics

A gymnastics competition is called a **meet**. Gymnasts perform **routines** on pieces of equipment during a meet. The equipment Jahn created is still used in competitive gymnastics today.

Gymnasts also compete on newer equipment, such as **still rings** and **uneven bars**. Judges watch each routine and give each gymnast a score. Gymnasts who perform difficult routines well get the most points.

! **fun fact**
Gymnastics became a sport in the Olympics for men in 1896 and for women in 1928.

Gymnasts perform tumbling routines on a square mat during the **floor exercise**. Springs and foam are underneath the mat. They help gymnasts jump high and perform flips and twists.

Women perform their floor exercise routines to music. This makes the routines more exciting.

Gymnasts often jump or flip off of a piece of equipment at the end of their routines. These are called **dismounts**.

Judges look for a perfect dismount to end a great routine. A gymnast who makes a perfect dismount is said to "stick the landing."

Gymnasts compete on each piece of equipment. They also compete against each other in the **all-around competition**. To find the winner, judges add up the gymnasts' scores from their routines on each piece of equipment. The gymnast with the highest total score wins the all-around competition. A gymnast needs strength, skill, and balance to win!

Gymnastics Gear

Gymnasts run, jump, and flip a lot.
They often perform dangerous moves.

Coaches keep gymnasts safe by teaching them in a gym with soft mats on the floor. Gymnasts can tumble and fall on the mats without getting hurt.

Female gymnasts wear leotards. Males wear leotards without sleeves called singlets with shorts or long pants.

Gymnasts also wear hand grips to protect their hands while they hold on to bars or rings. Gymnasts rub chalk onto the hand grips to make it easier to hold on to equipment as they perform.

Shawn Johnson

Young gymnasts learn gymnastics at local gyms. Older gymnasts can join school gymnastics teams. The world's best gymnasts compete in the **Olympics**.

Nastia Liukin

fun fact

Nastia Liukin won the gold medal in the all-around competition at the 2008 Olympics in Beijing, China.

U.S. gymnasts Shawn Johnson and Nastia Liukin thrill fans around the world. Their skills and routines have led them to win several championships. The sport of gymnastics continues to change as the world's top gymnasts learn new skills and perform exciting new routines.

Glossary

all-around competition—a competition to determine the best gymnast at a meet

balance beam—a piece of gymnastics equipment that is made up of a long, narrow beam that gymnasts balance on while doing routines

dismount—jumping or flipping off of gymnastics equipment at the end of a routine

flexibility—the ability to easily bend and stretch

floor exercise—a gymnastics routine during which a gymnast performs a tumbling routine on a large mat

high bar—a piece of gymnastics equipment that is made up of a single raised bar that gymnasts flip over

meet—a gymnastics competition

Olympics—a worldwide sporting event held every four years

parallel bars—a piece of gymnastics equipment that is made up of two raised bars of the same height that gymnasts flip around

routine—a gymnastics performance

still rings—a piece of gymnastics equipment that is made up of two rings hanging from the ceiling on which gymnasts perform

uneven bars—a piece of gymnastics equipment that is made up of two bars placed next to each other at different heights

vault—a piece of gymnastics equipment that is made up of a raised surface that gymnasts run up to and flip over

To Learn More

AT THE LIBRARY

Bray-Moffatt, Naia. *I Love Gymnastics*. New York, N.Y.: DK Publishing, 2005.

Morley, Christine. *The Best Book of Gymnastics*. New York, N.Y.: Kingfisher, 2003.

Patterson, Carly and Clint Kelly. *Carly Patterson: Be Strong*. Kirkland, Wash.: Positively for Kids, 2006.

ON THE WEB

Learning more about gymnastics is as easy as 1, 2, 3.

1. Go to www.factsurfer.com.

2. Enter "gymnastics" into the search box.

3. Click the "Surf" button and you will see a list of related Web sites.

With factsurfer.com, finding more information is just a click away.

Index

The images in this book are reproduced through the courtesy of: Jiang Dao Hua, front cover; Brian Pieters / Masterfile, pp. 4-5, 13; Lars Baron / Getty Images, p. 6; Dominique Douieb / Getty Images, p. 7; Alistair Berg / Getty Images, p. 8; Valeria 73, p. 9; Jed Jacobsohn / Getty Images, p. 10; Matt Dunham / Associated Press, p. 11; Rob Carr, Associated Press, p. 12; Zoran Milich / Getty Images, pp. 14-15; AFP / Stringer/ Getty Images, p. 16; Al Bello / Staff / Getty Images, p. 17; Graham French / Masterfile, p. 18; Image Source / Getty Images, p. 19; Rob Carr / Associated Press, p. 20; Julie Jacobson, p. 21.